STEAM TRAINS

© Werner & Hansjörg Brutzer

Published by
Dirk Stursberg Publishing
www.dirkstursberg.com

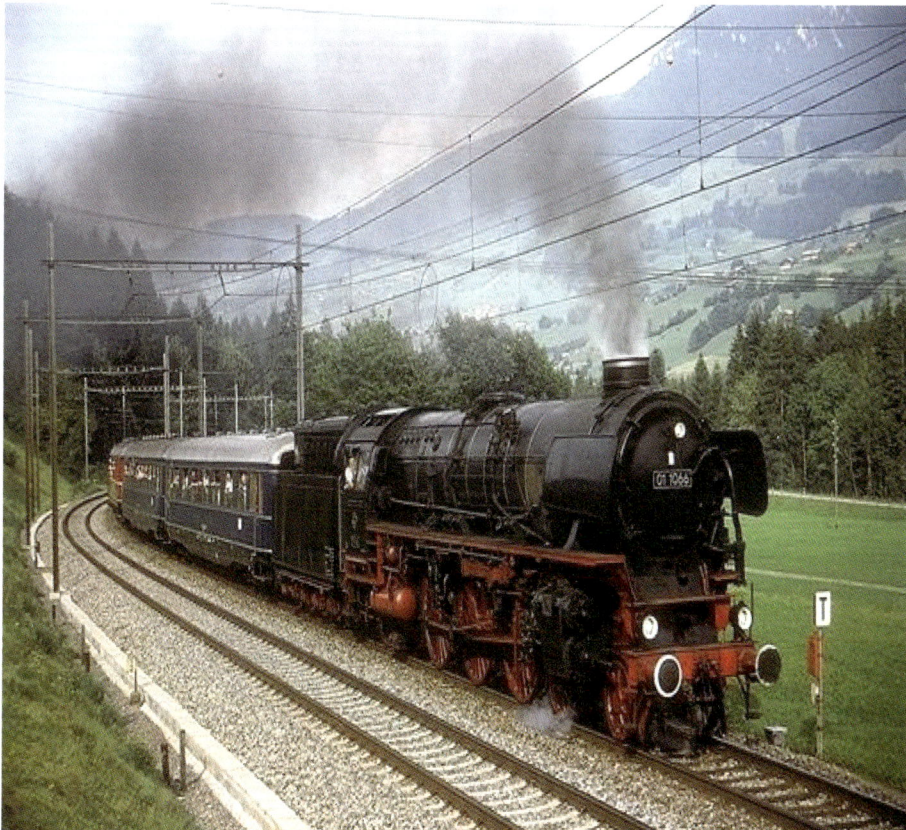

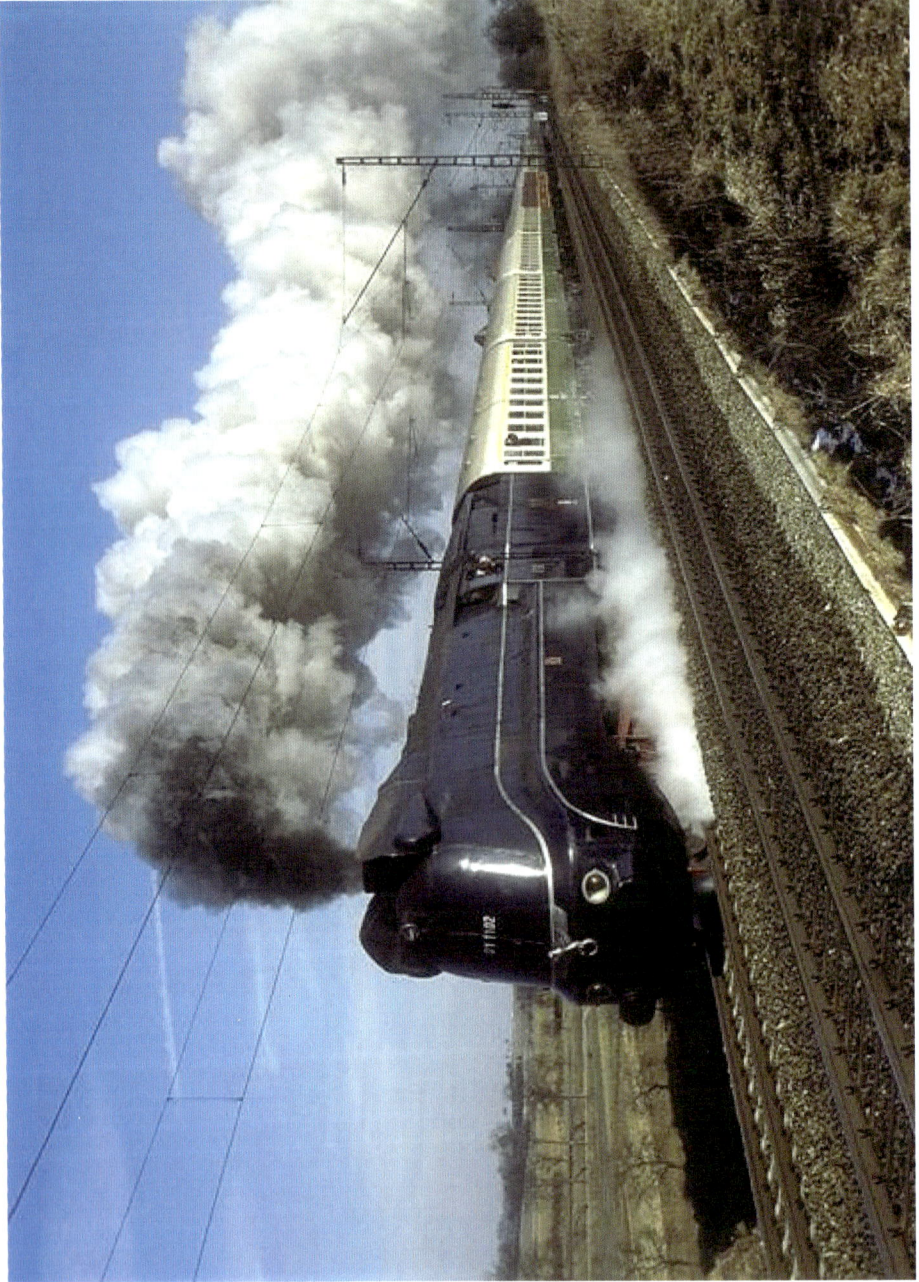

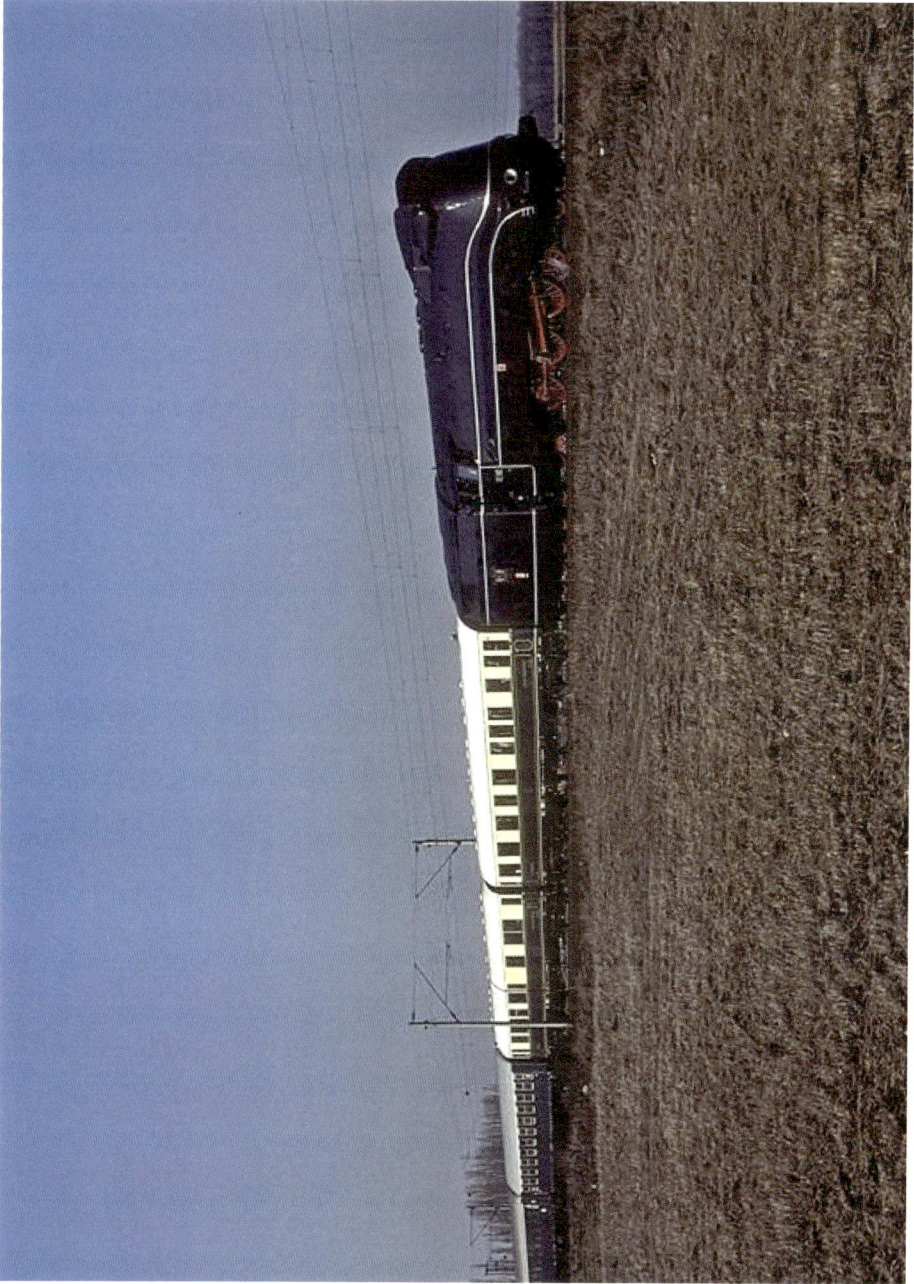

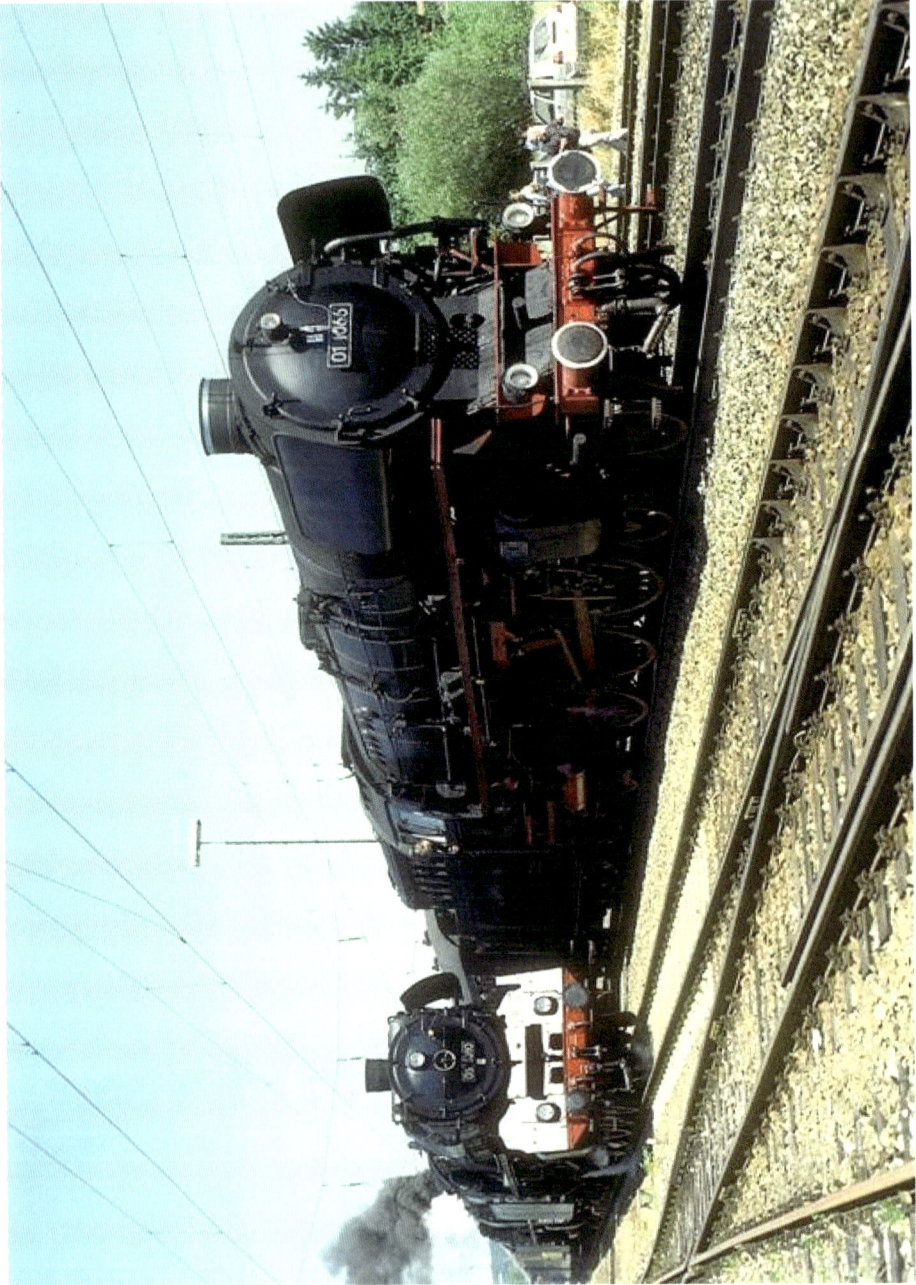

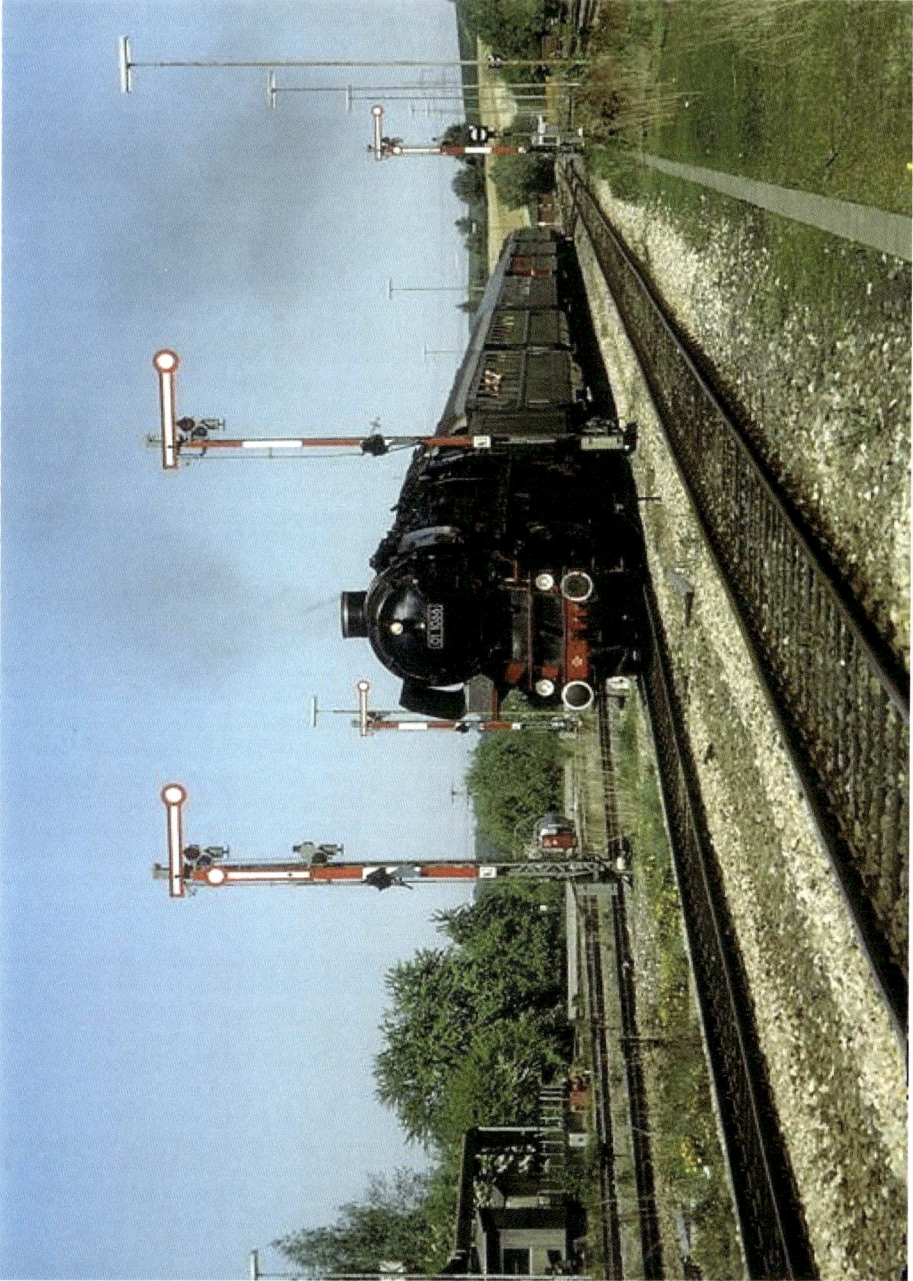

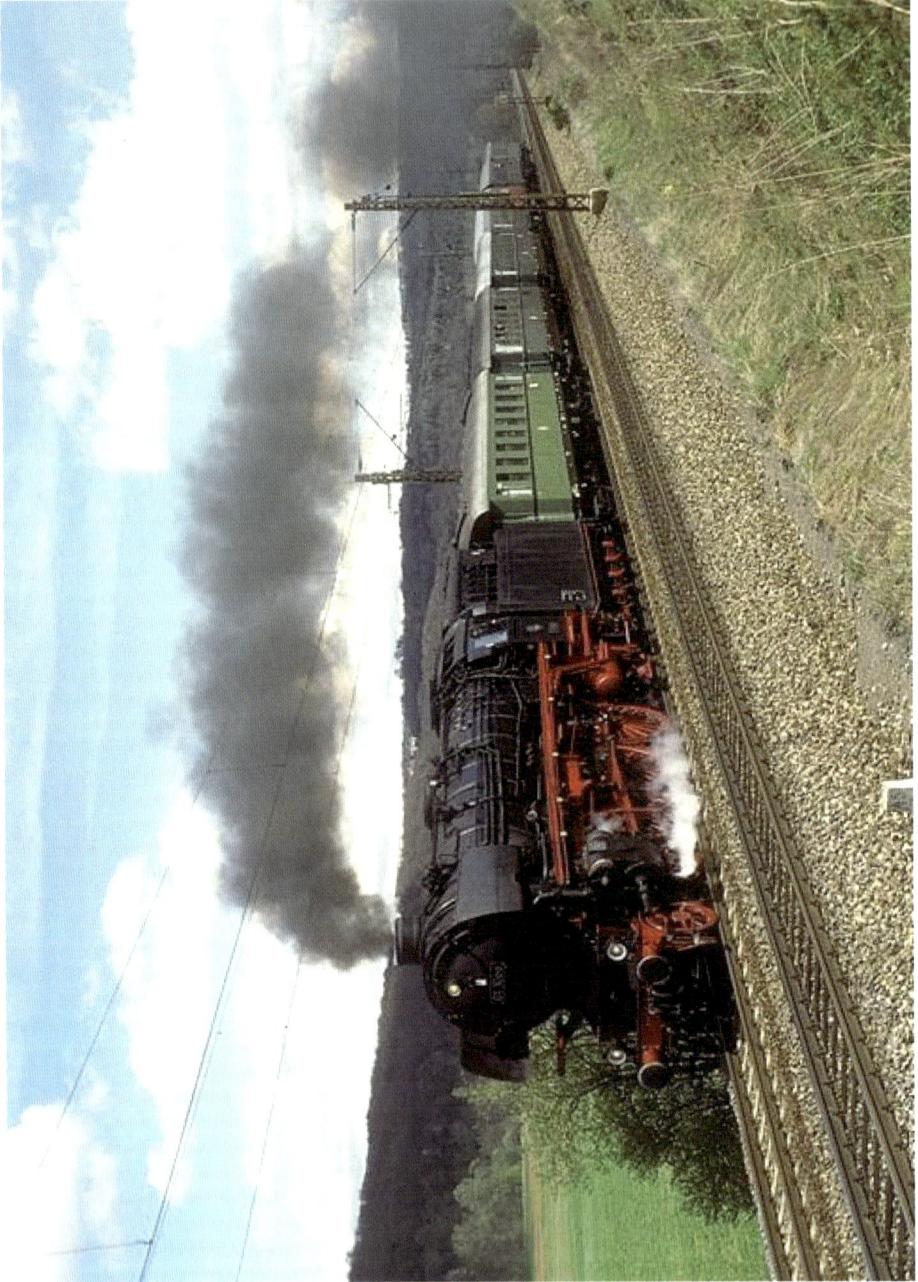

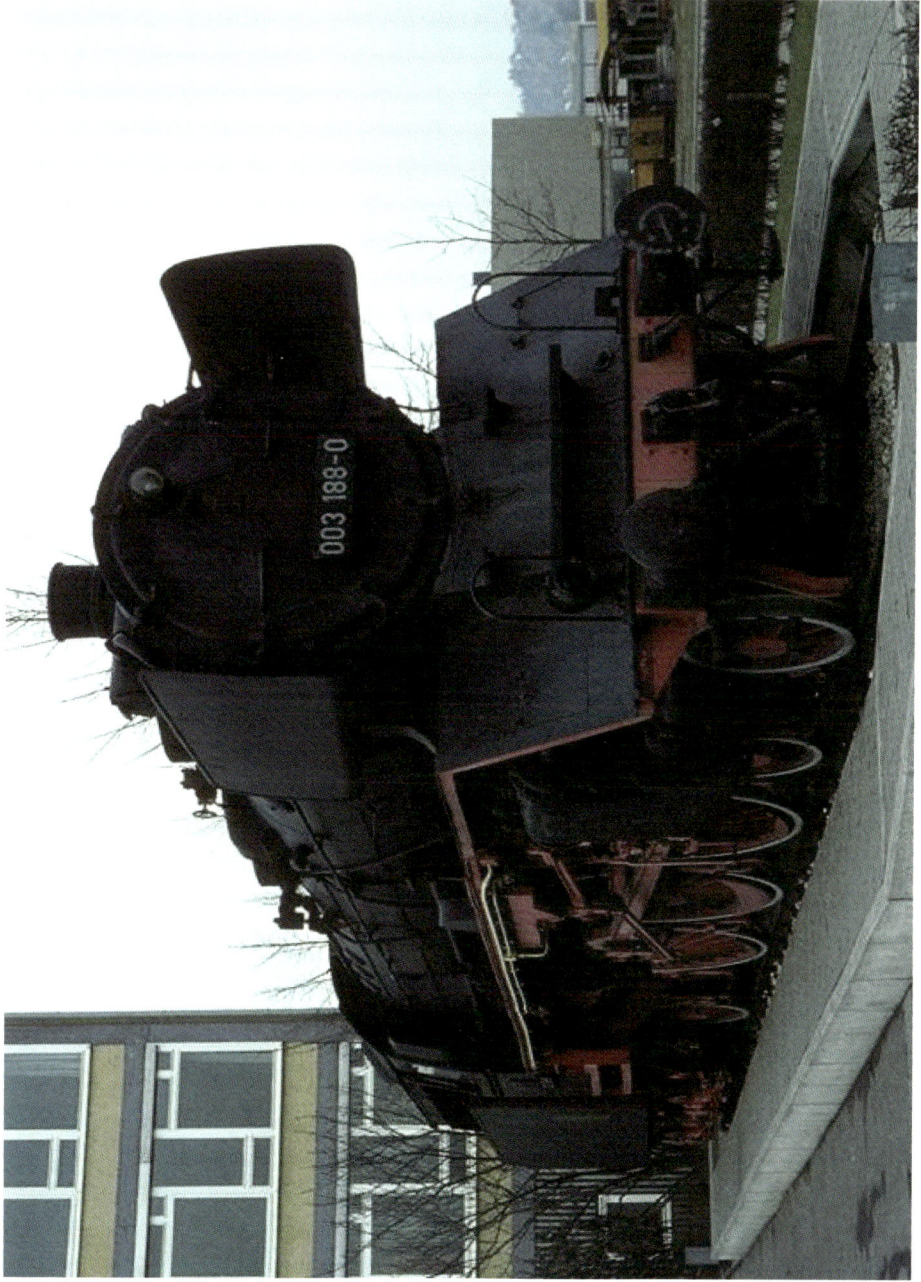

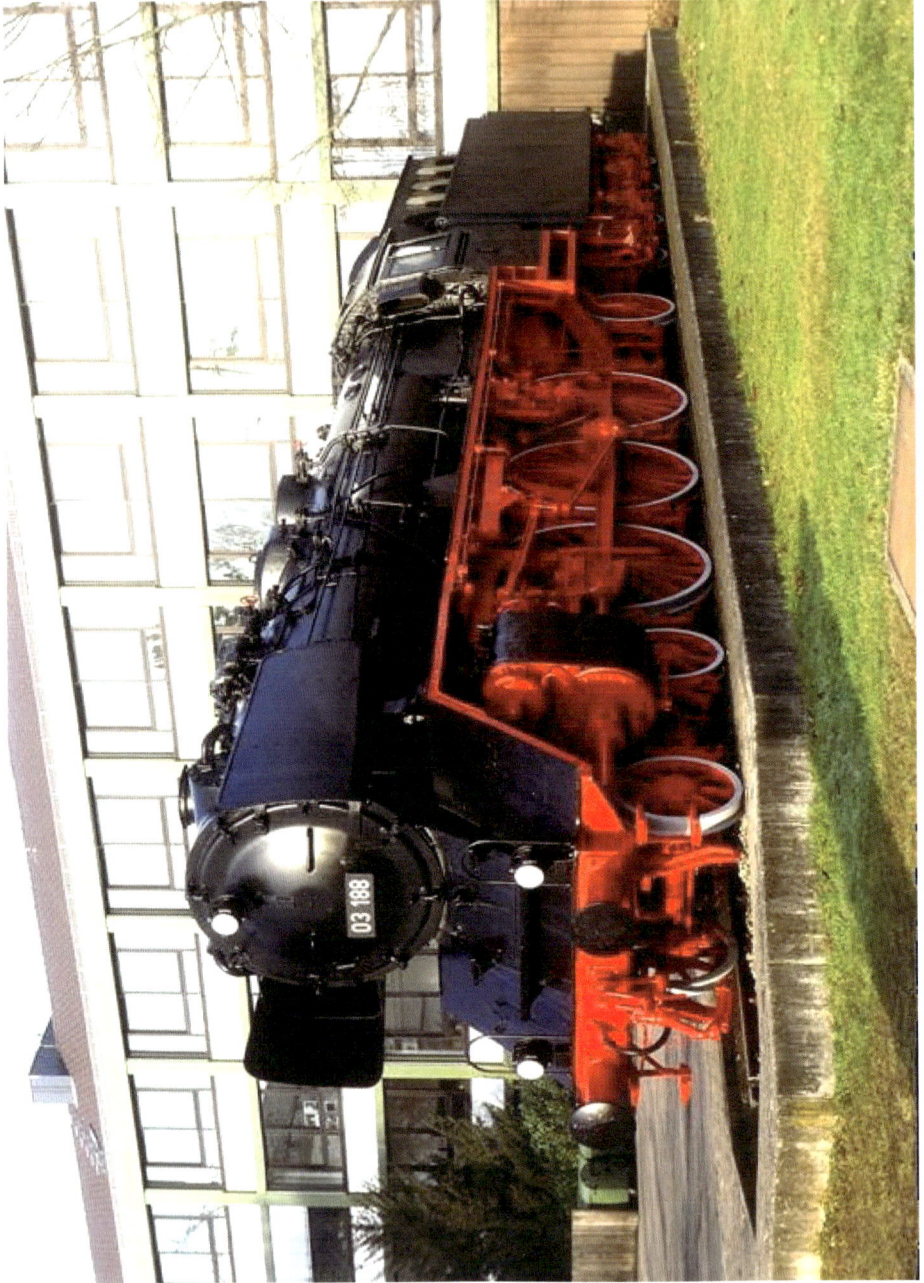

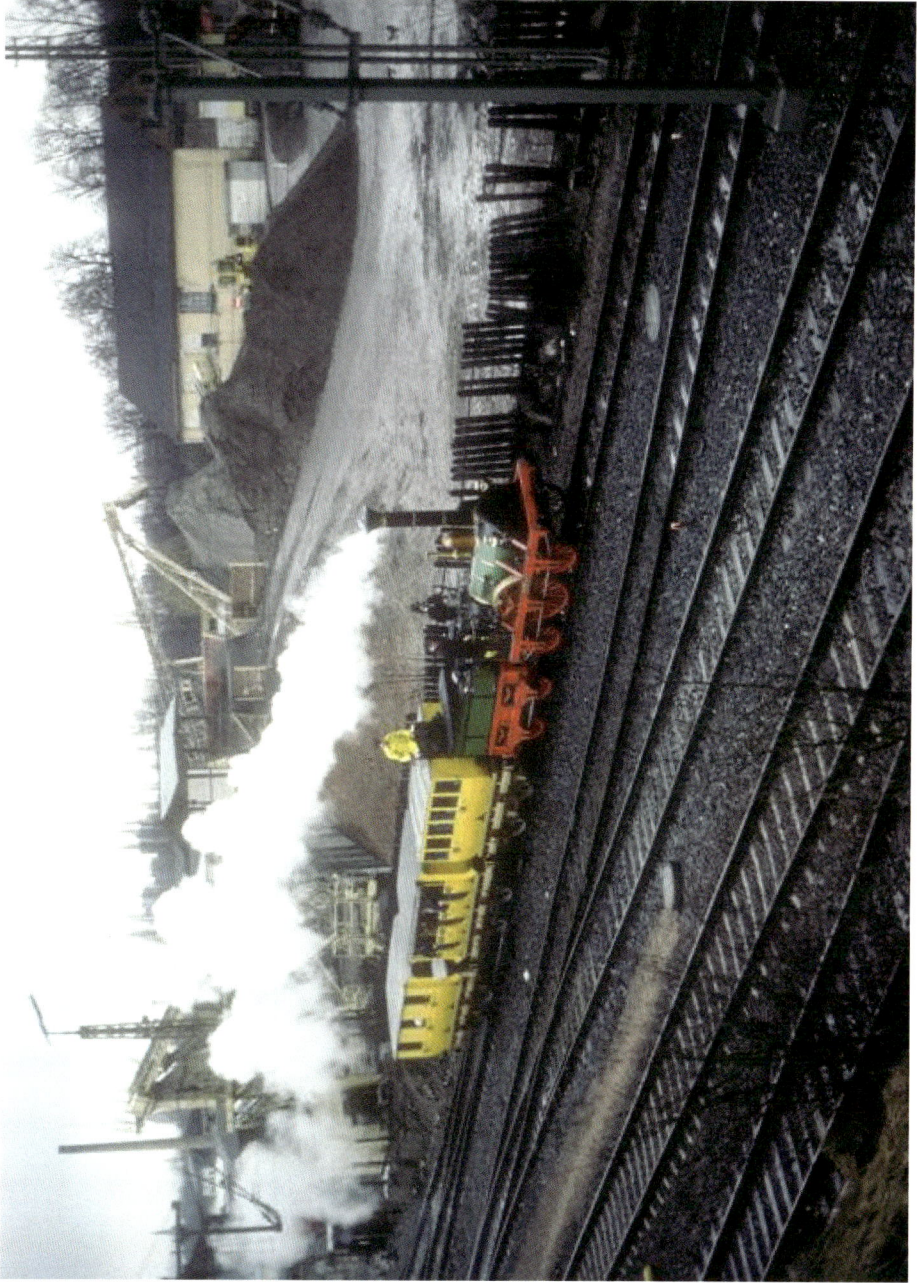

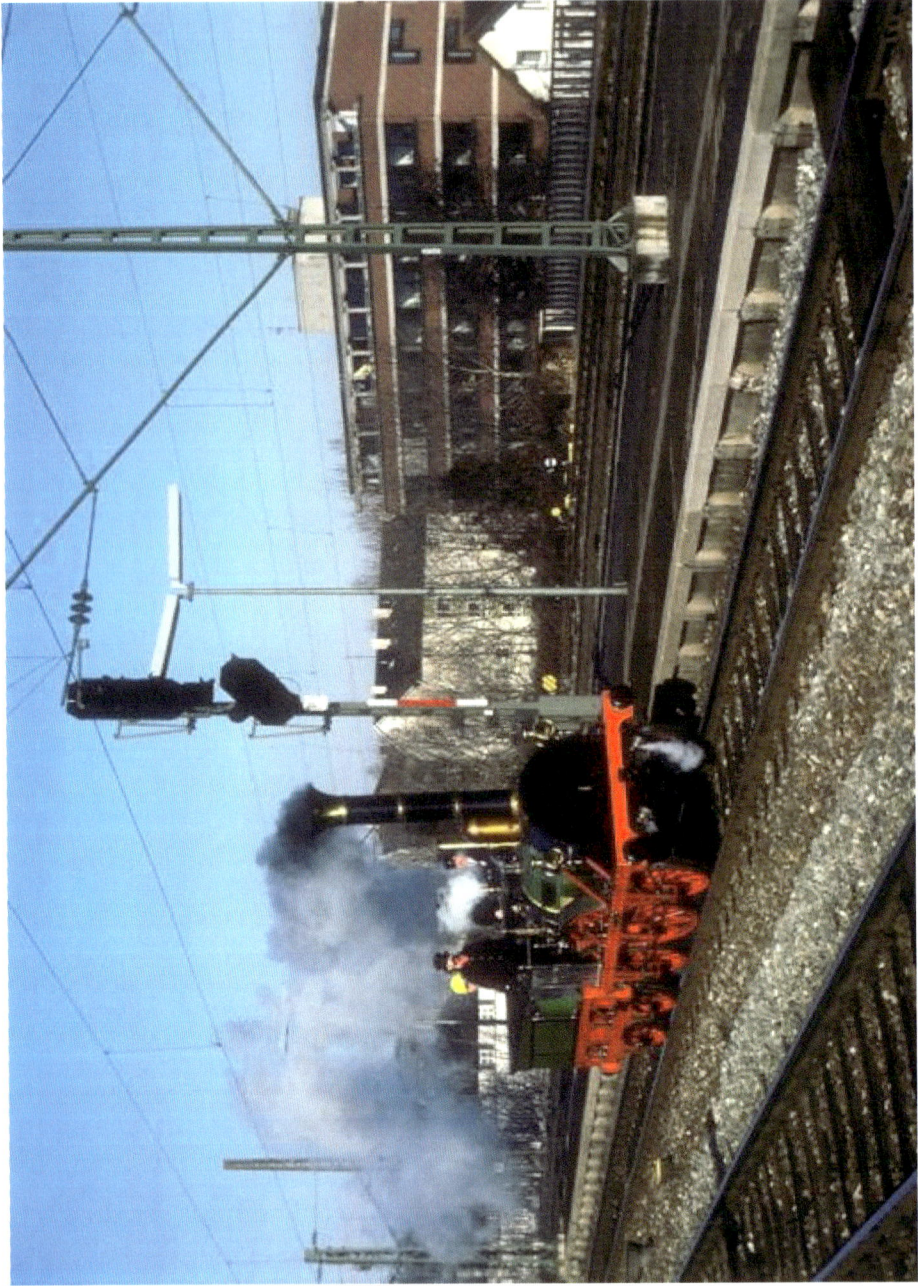

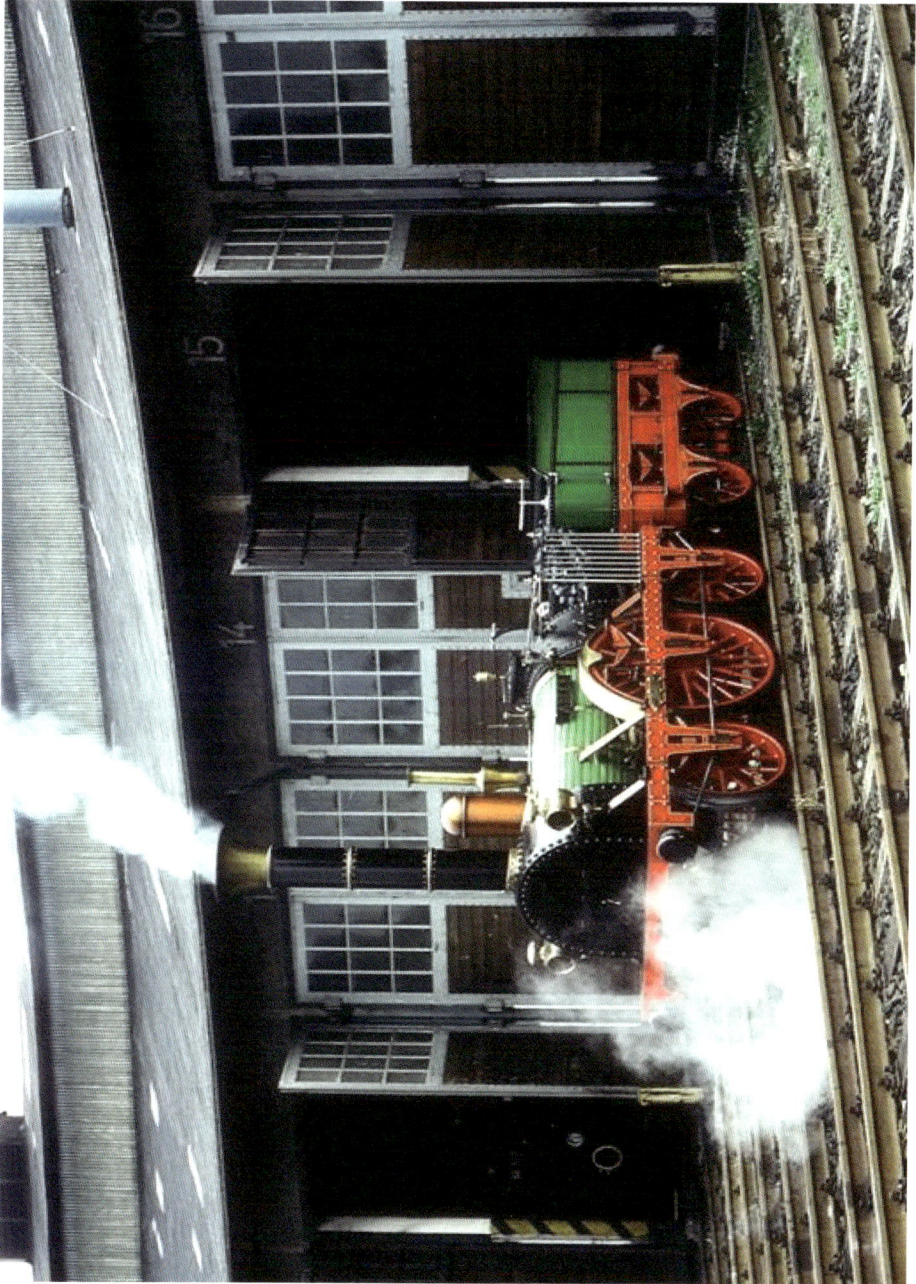

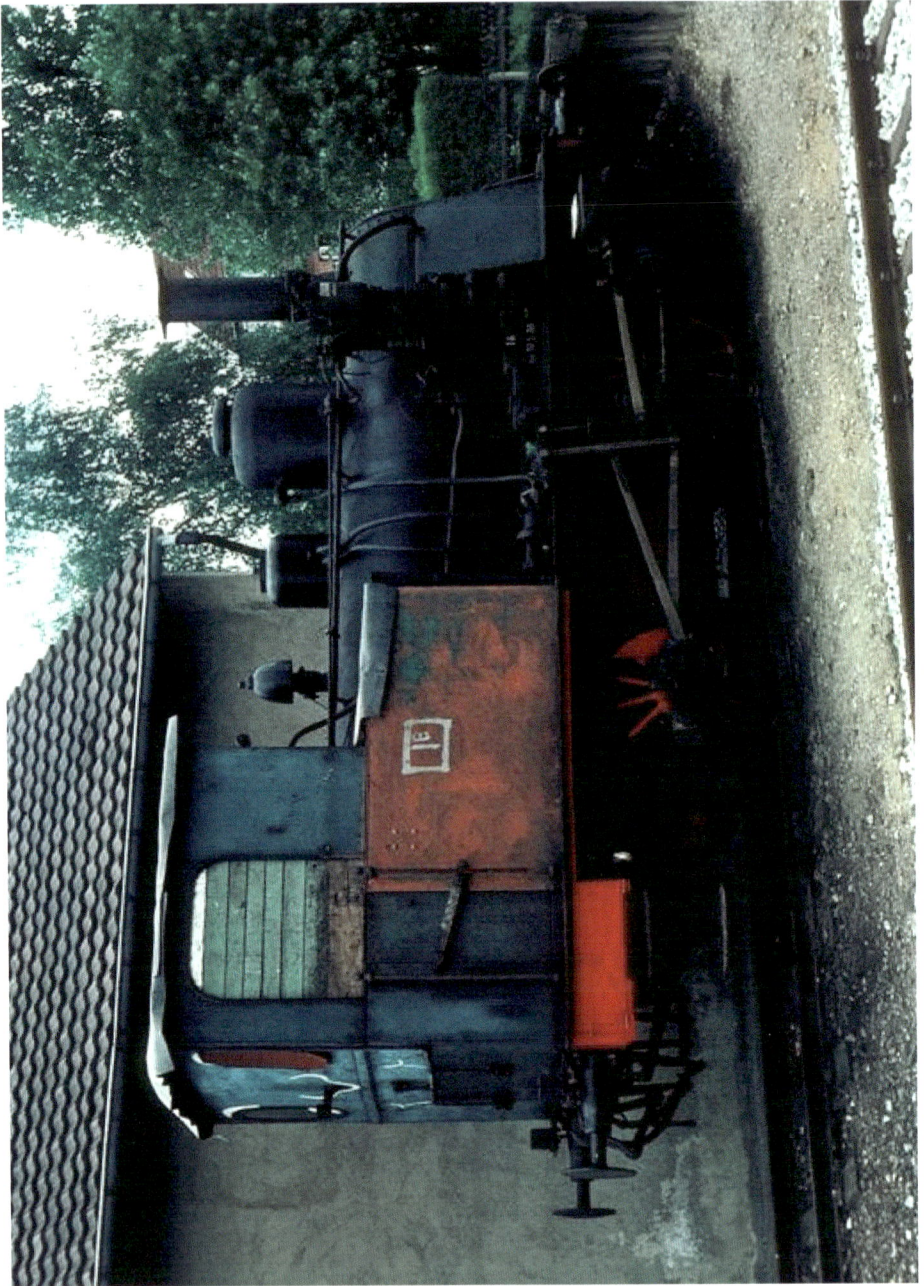

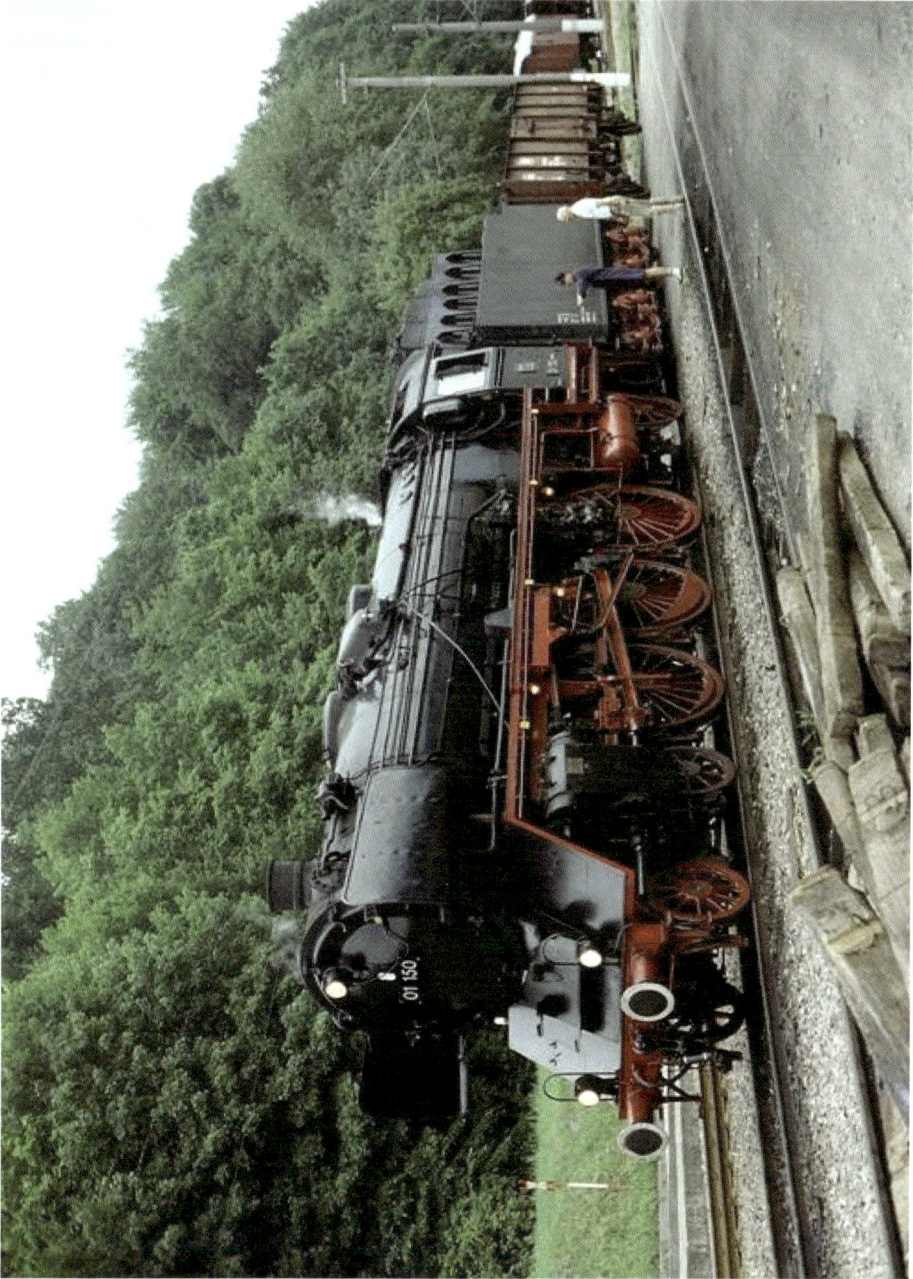

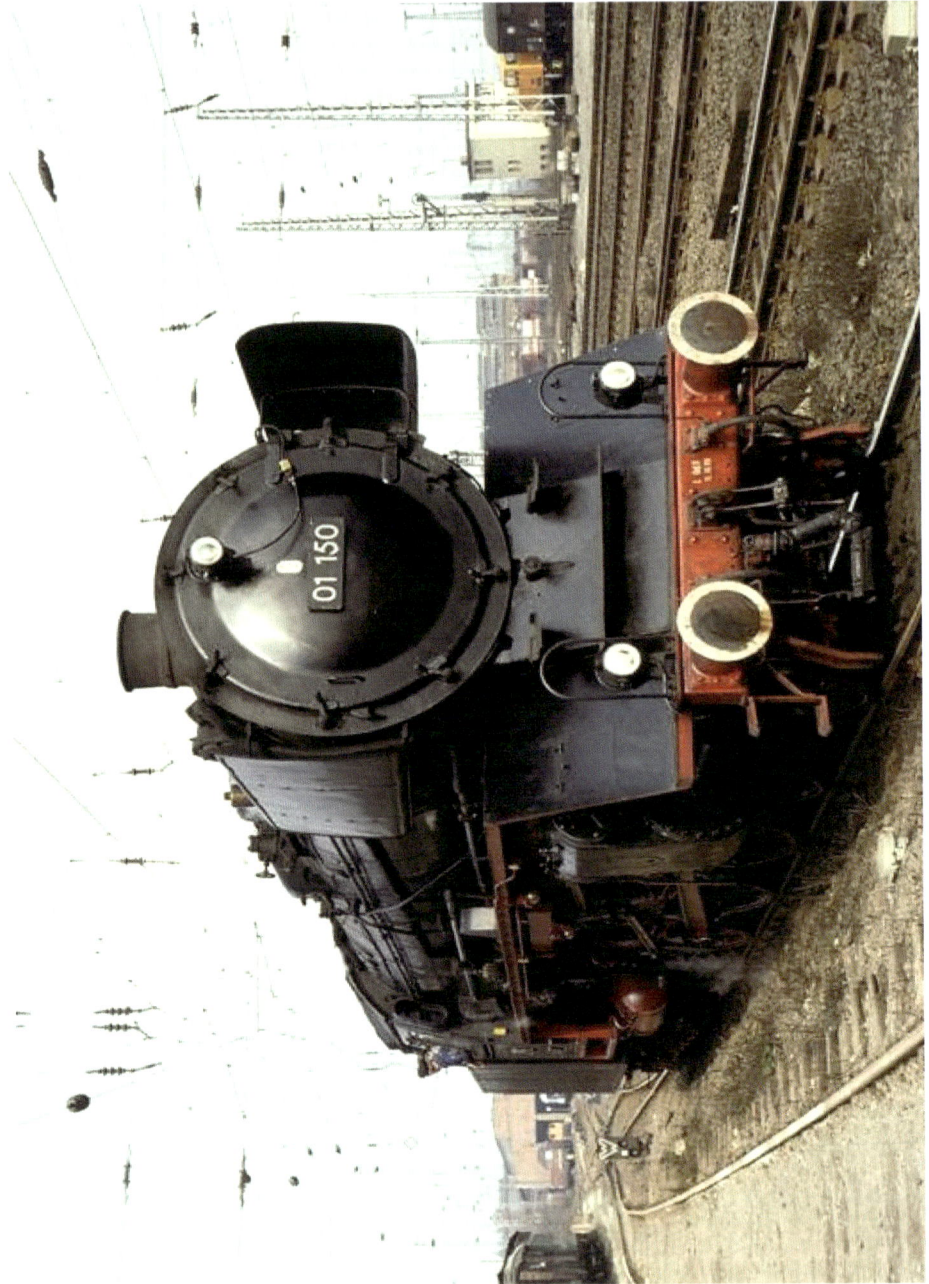

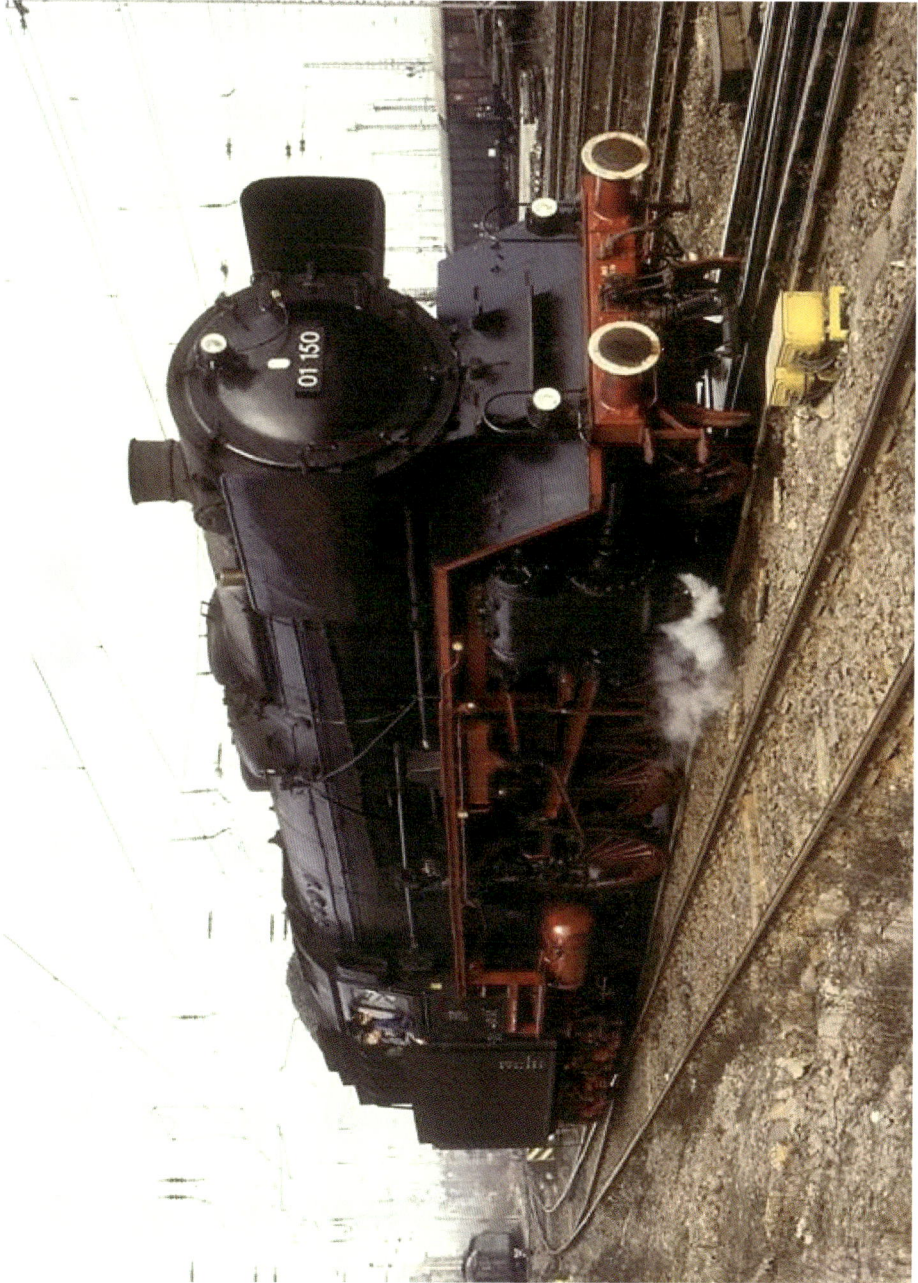

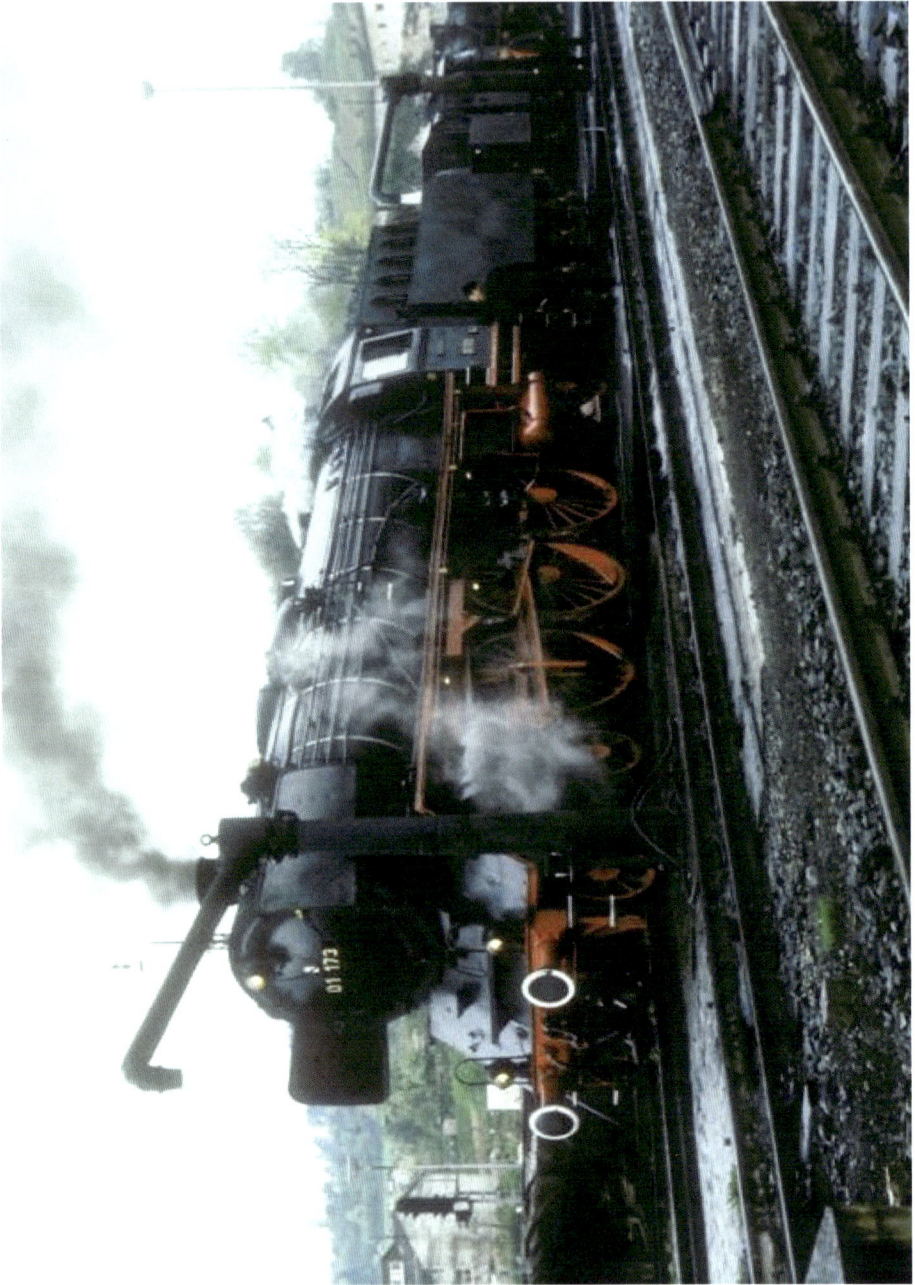

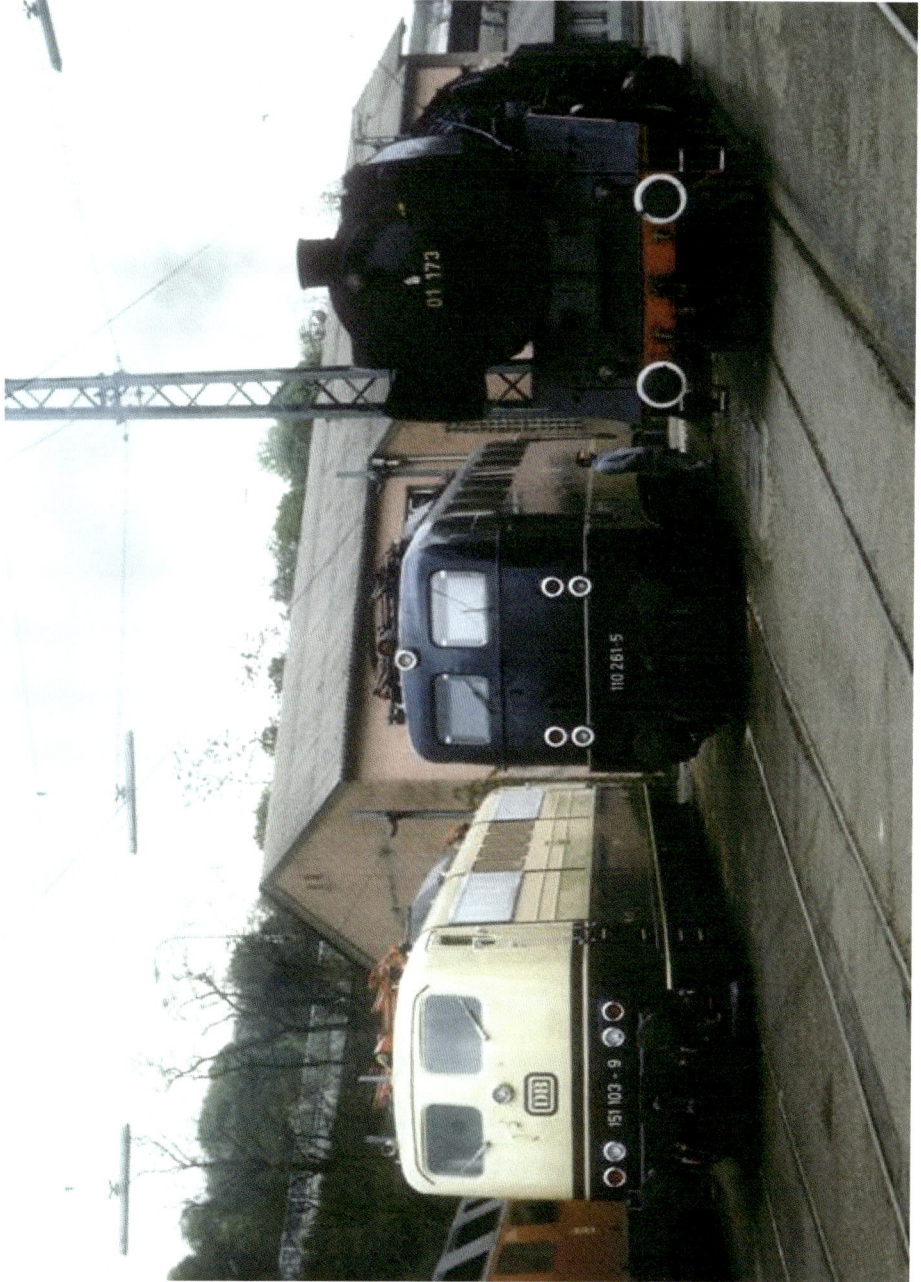

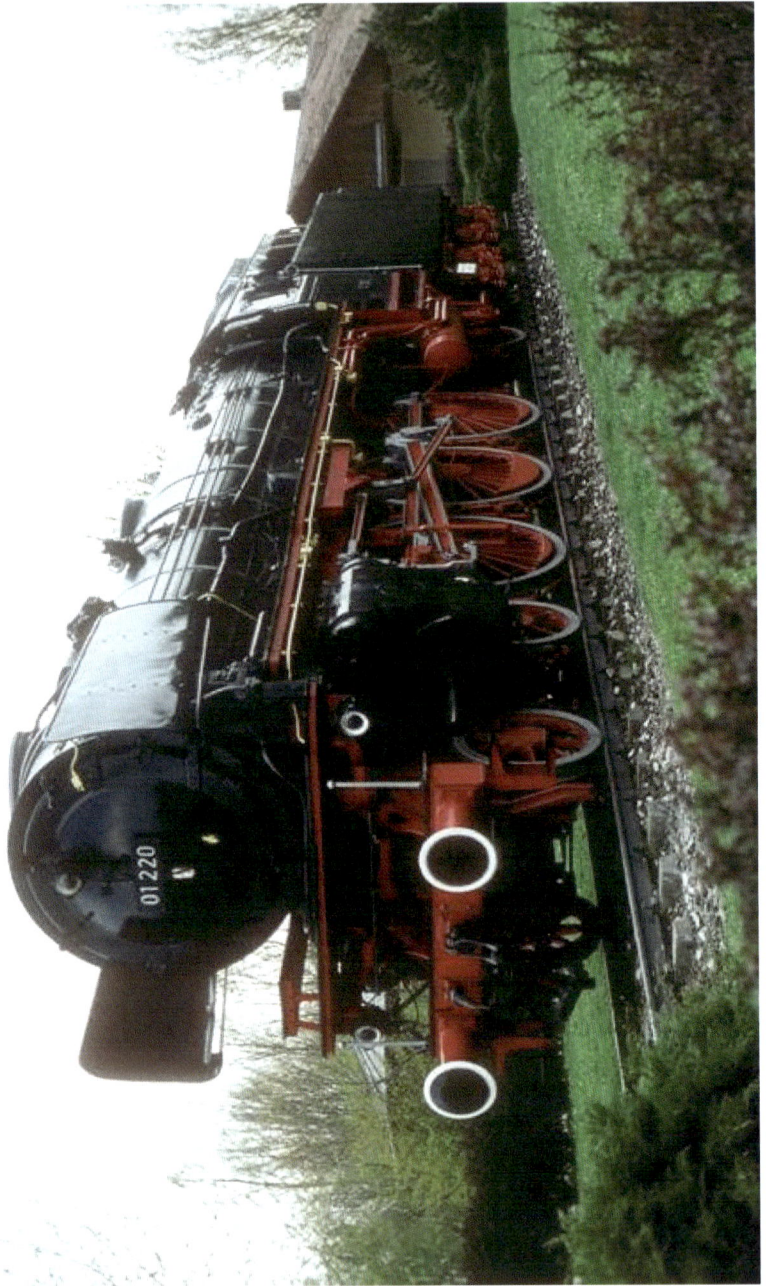

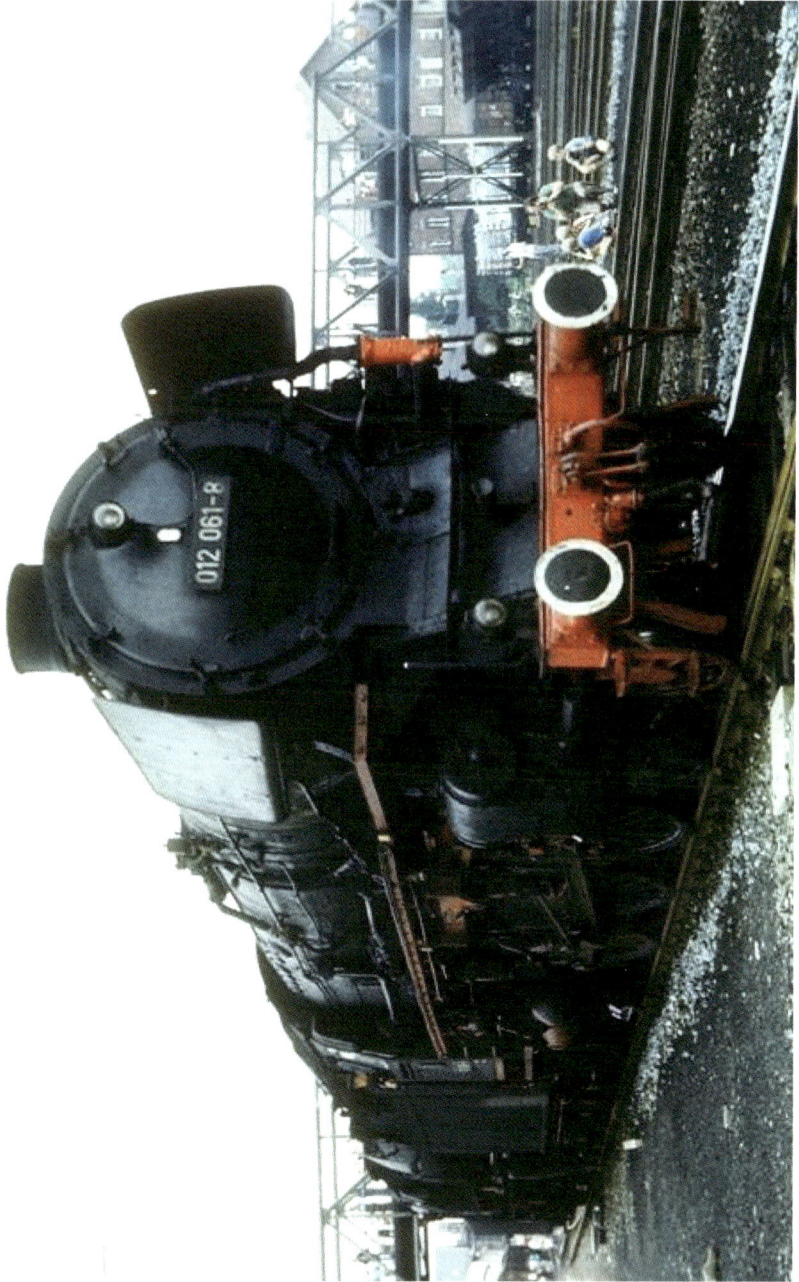

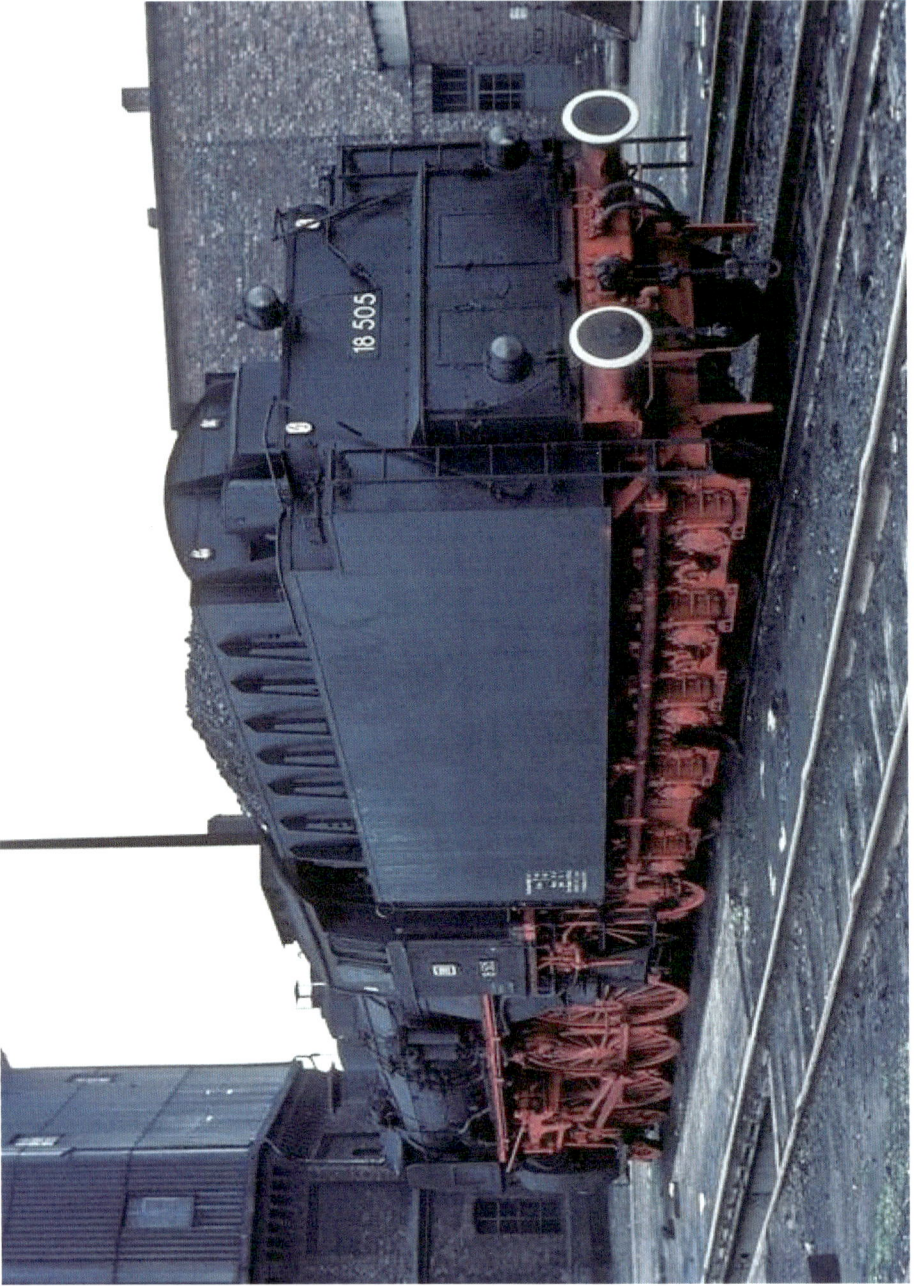

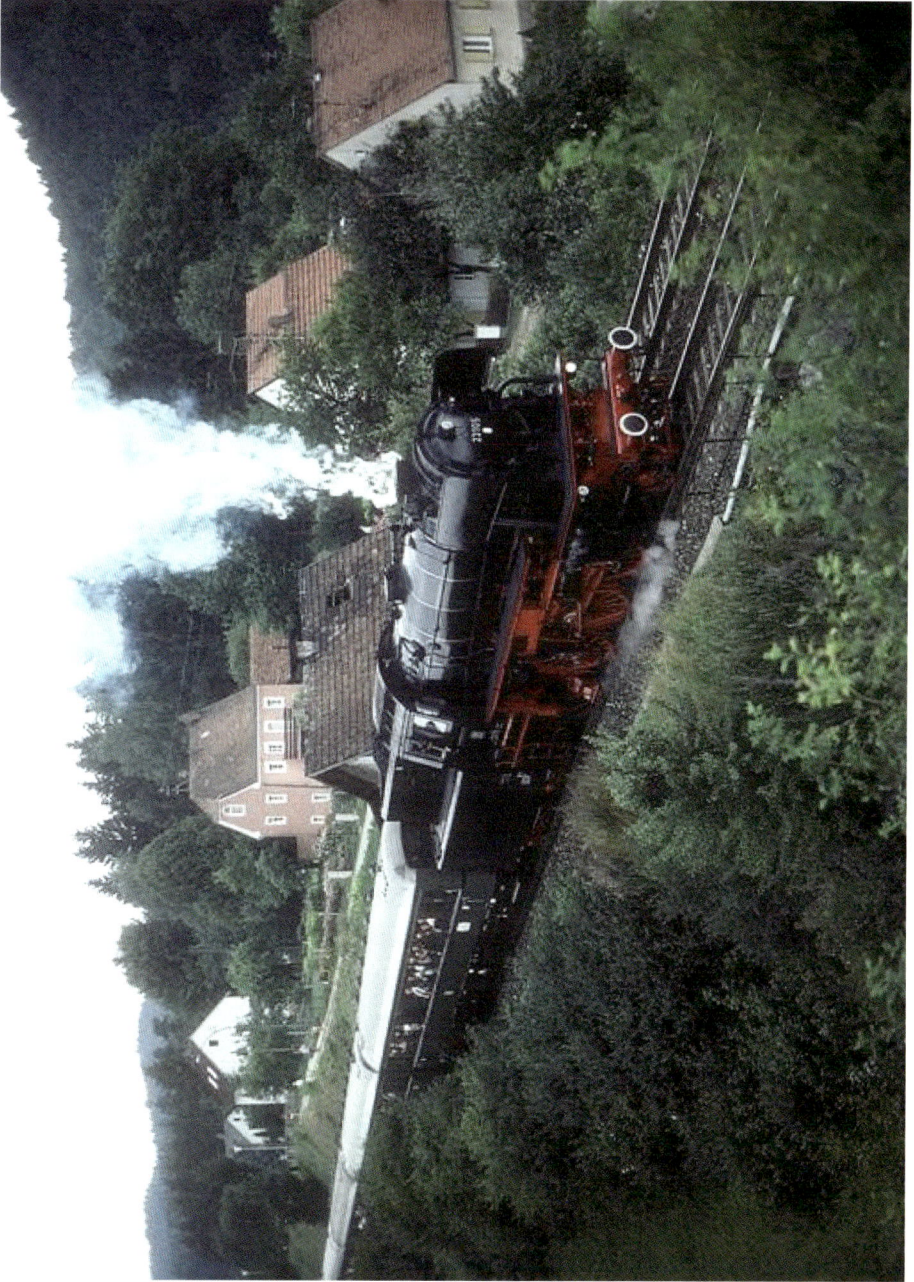

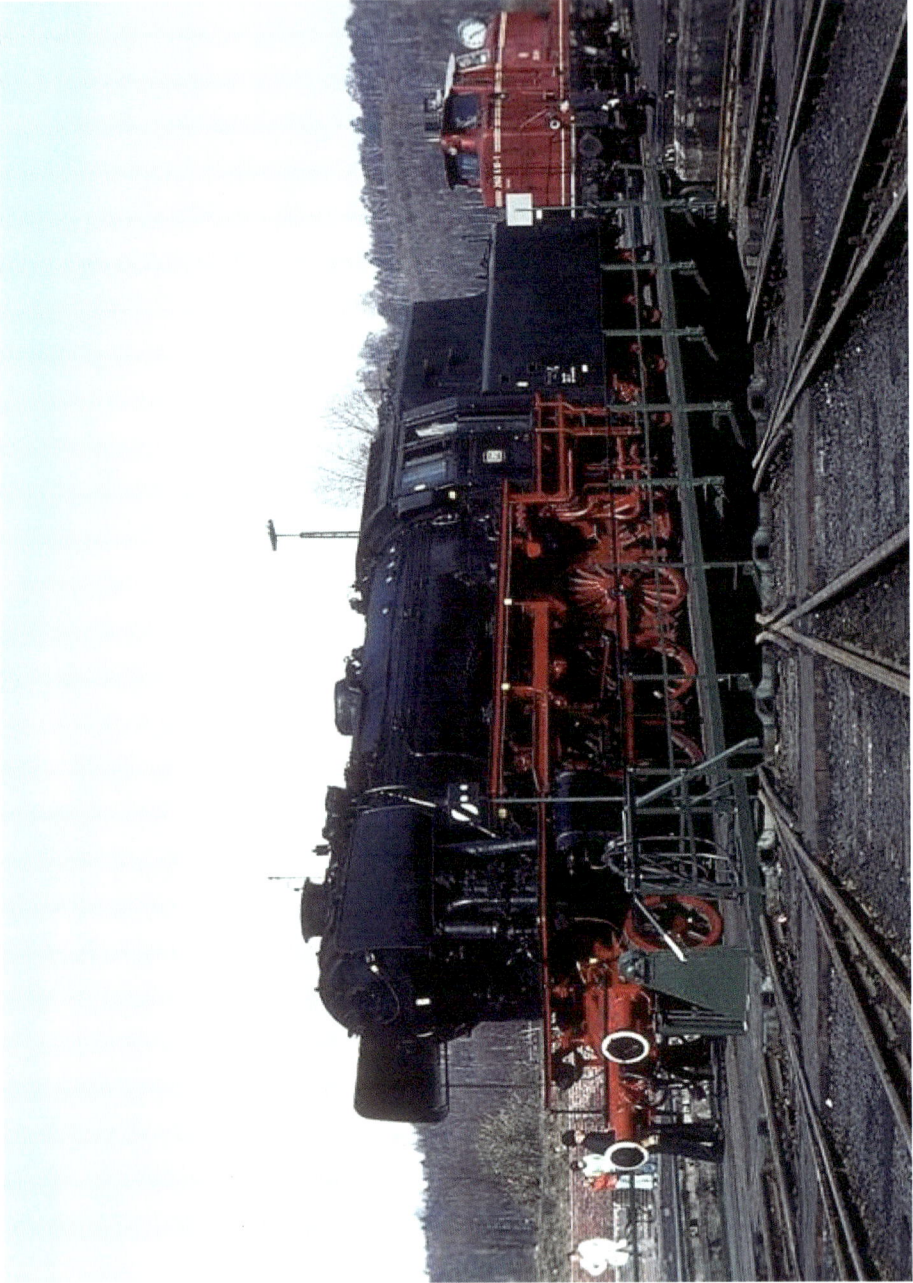

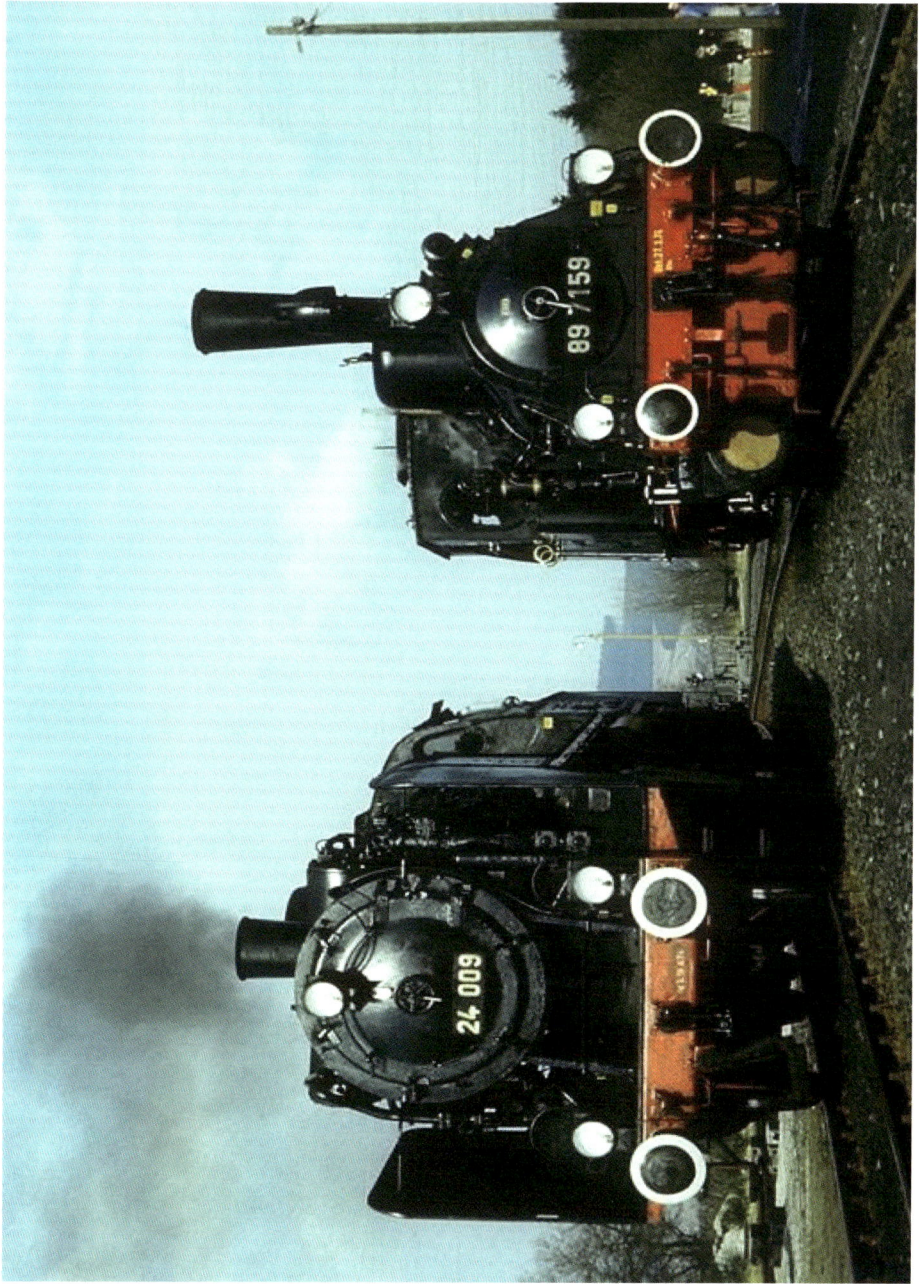

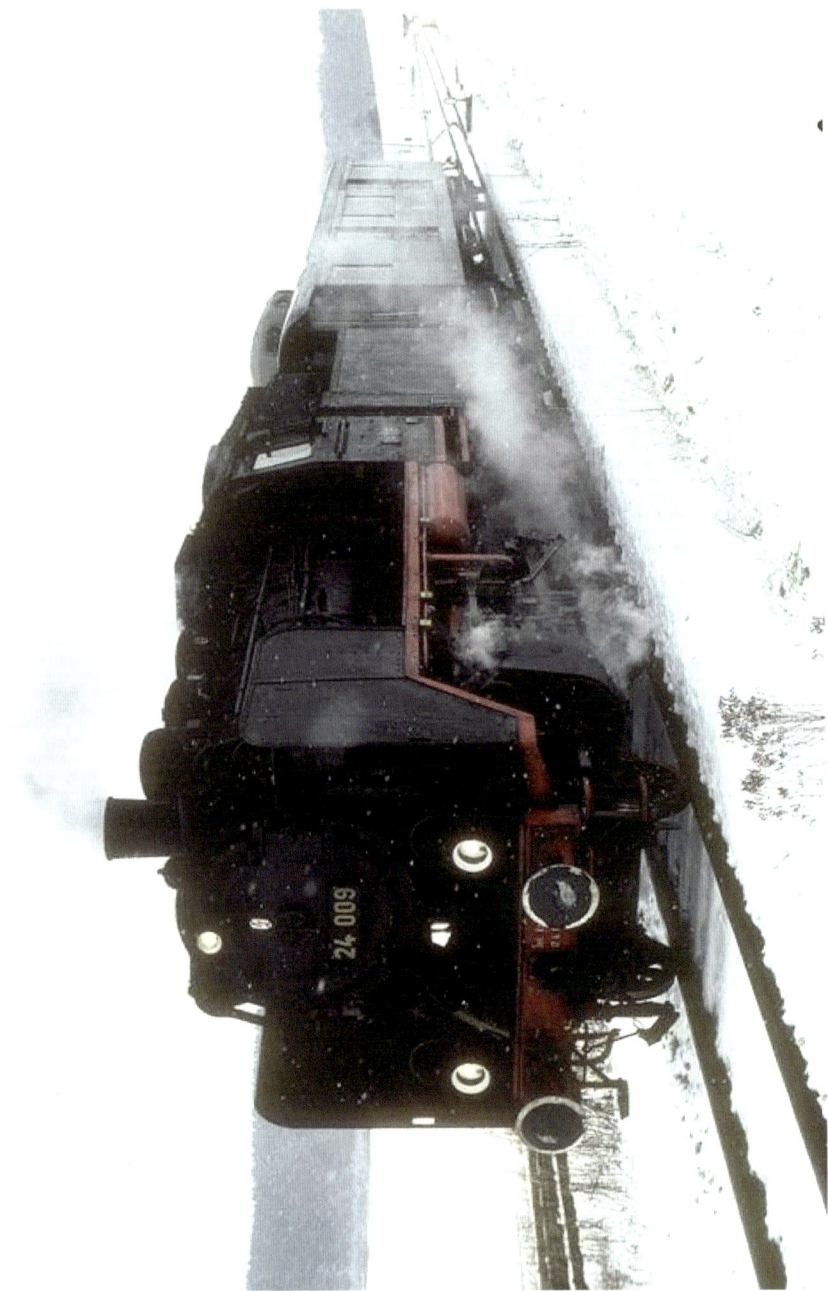

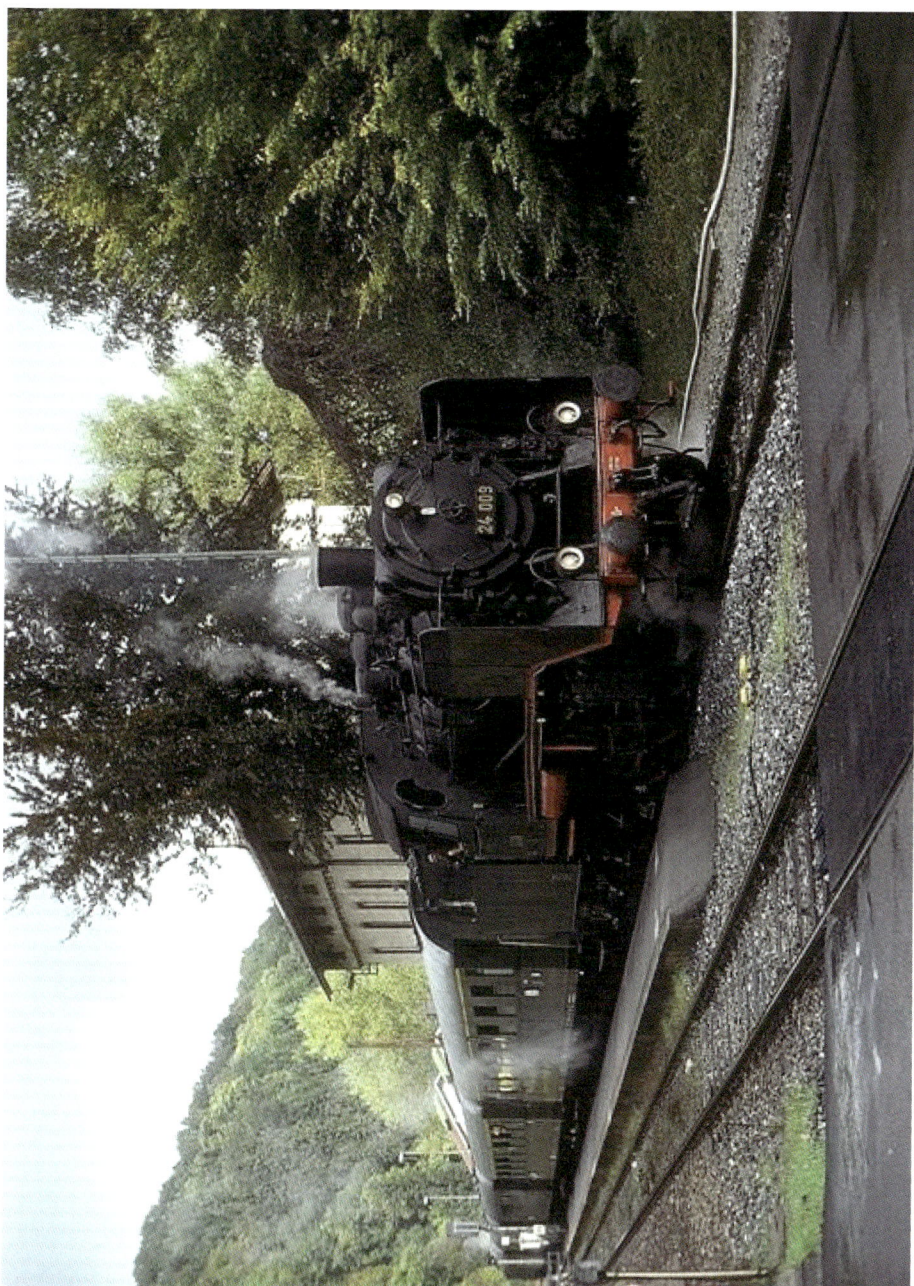

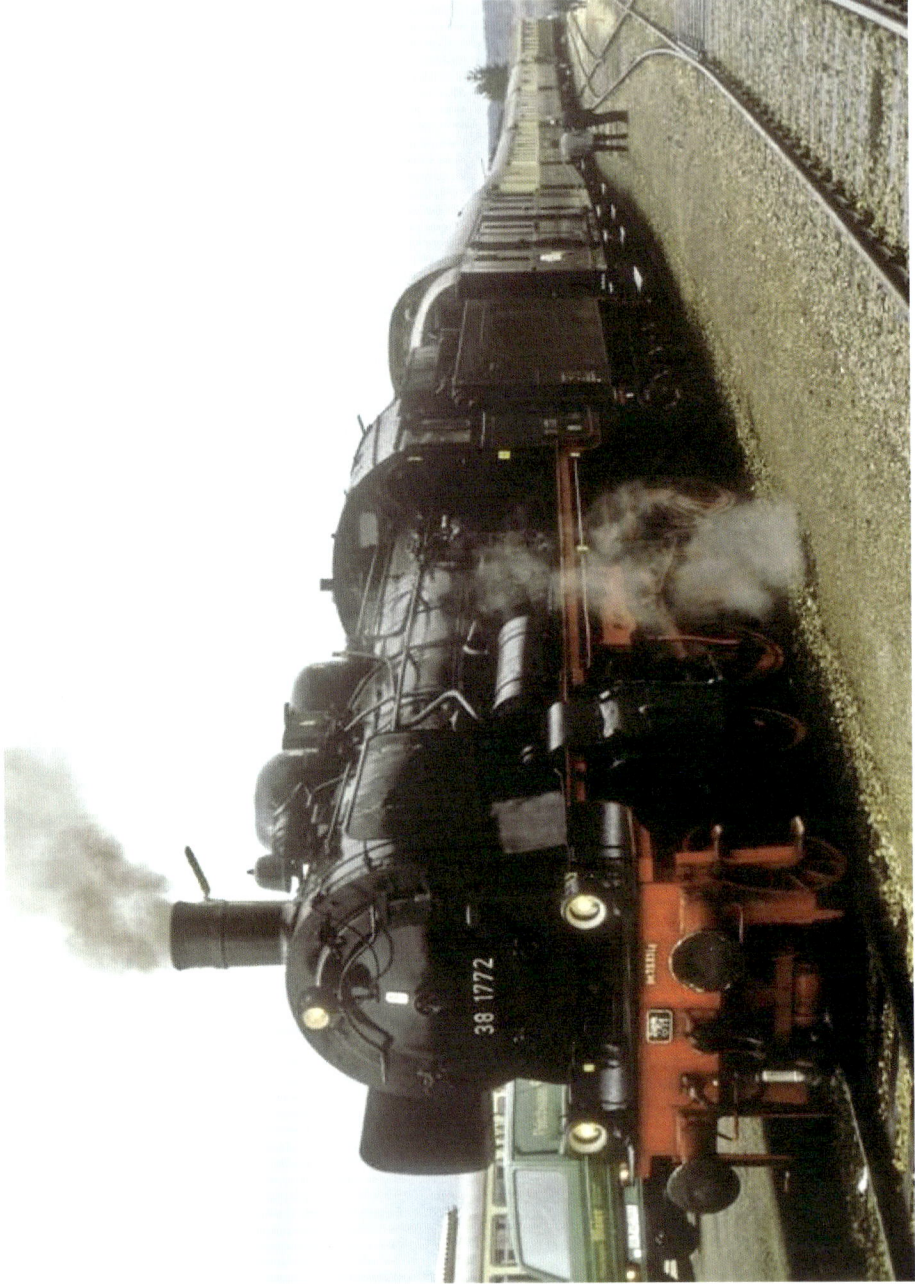

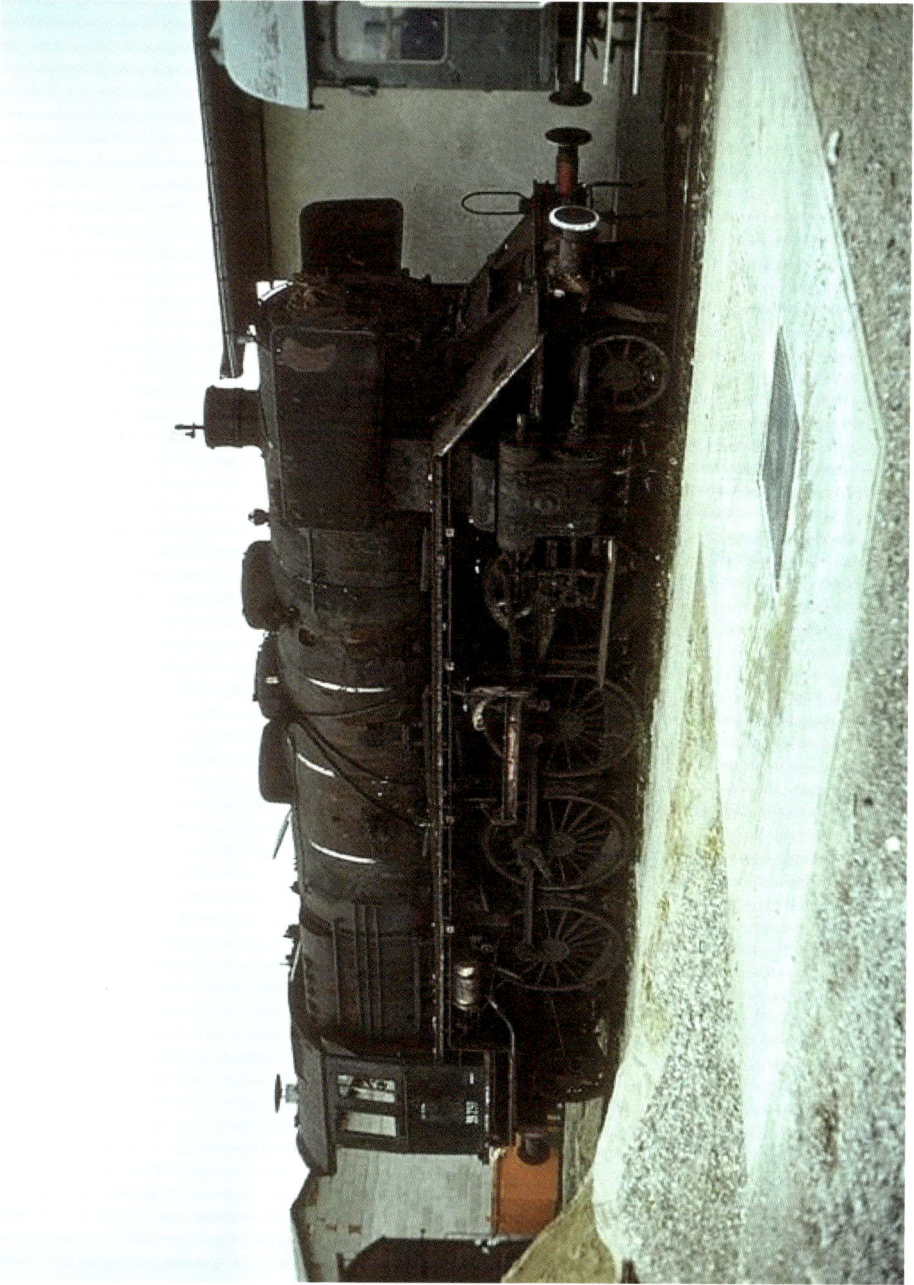

CPSIA information can be obtained at www.ICGtesting.com
Printed in the USA
LVIW01n2257060817
544061LV00005B/17